page 29

Loving Promises
especially for you

By Helen Steiner Rice

"Promises
Divinely
Spoken
Remain
Unfailing
and Unbroken"

Loving Promises

especially for you

Helen Steiner Rice

Fleming H. Revell Company
Old Tappan, New Jersey

Scripture quotations, unless otherwise identified, are from the
King James Version of the Bible.

Scripture quotations identified RSV are from the Revised Standard
Version of the Bible, copyrighted 1946, 1952, ©1971 and 1973.

Library of Congress Cataloging in Publication Data

Rice, Helen Steiner.
  Loving promises : especially for you.

  Poems.
  I. Title.
PS 3568.I28L58   811'.5'4   75-4765
ISBN 0-8007-0736-2
ISBN 0-8007-0737-0 Keepsake

Contents

And this is what he has promised us, eternal life.

1 John 2:25 RSV

The Promises of Man May Fail but God's Promises Prevail

In this uncertain world of trouble
With its sorrow, sin and strife
Man needs a haven for his heart
To endure the "storms of life"...
He keeps hoping for a promise
Of better, bigger things
With the power and the prestige
That fame and fortune brings...
And the world is rife with promises
That are fast and falsely spoken
For man in his deceptive way
Knows his promise can be broken...
But when GOD makes a promise
It remains forever true
For everything GOD promises
He unalterably will do...
So read the promises of GOD
That will never fail or falter
And inherit EVERLASTING LIFE
Which even death can't alter...
And when you're disillusioned
And every hope is blighted
Recall the promises of GOD
And your FAITH will be relighted,
Knowing there's ONE LASTING PROMISE
On which man can depend,
And that's the PROMISE of SALVATION
And a LIFE THAT HAS NO END.

Preface

One of the happy surprises in reading the poems of Helen Steiner Rice is discovering old certainties expressed in new words. Again and again you have the feeling that you have heard something like this before. Chances are that you have—from the Bible.

In this new collection of Mrs. Rice's poems, her heart-touching lines are mingled with verses from Holy Writ. Here are assurance and affirmation, counsel and comfort, unforgettable poems and incomparable promises.

As the author herself has written,
"...the words that never fail us
Are the words of God above."

We take great pleasure in presenting this very special book for your enjoyment and inspiration.

The Publishers

If we live in the Spirit, let us also walk in the Spirit.

Galatians 5:25

Love does no wrong to a neighbor; therefore love is the fulfilling of the law.

Romans 13:10   RSV

Where There Is Love

Where there is love the heart is light,
Where there is love the day is bright,
Where there is love there is a song
To help when things are going wrong,
Where there is love there is a smile
To make all things seem more worthwhile,
Where there is love there's quiet peace,
A tranquil place where turmoils cease...
Love changes darkness into light
And makes the heart take "wingless flight"—
Oh, blest are they who walk in love...
They also walk with God above,
And when man walks with God again
There shall be Peace On Earth for men.

And we know that all things work together
for good to them that love God....

Romans 8:28

God Knows Best

Our Father knows what's best for us,
So why should we complain—
We always want the sunshine,
But He knows there must be rain—
We love the sound of laughter
And the merriment of cheer,
But our hearts would lose their tenderness
If we never shed a tear...
Our Father tests us often
With suffering and with sorrow,
He tests us, not to punish us,
But to help us meet TOMORROW...
For growing trees are strengthened
When they withstand the storm,
And the sharp cut of the chisel
Gives the marble grace and form...
God never hurts us needlessly,
And He never wastes our pain,
For every loss He sends to us
Is followed by rich gain...
And when we count the blessings
That God has so freely sent,
We will find no cause for murmuring
And no time to lament...
For Our Father loves His children,
And to Him all things are plain,
So He never sends us PLEASURE
When the SOUL'S DEEP NEED IS PAIN...
So whenever we are troubled,
And when everything goes wrong,
It is just God working in us
To make OUR SPIRIT STRONG.

...when thou prayest, enter into thy closet, and when thou hast shut thy door, pray to thy Father which is in secret; and thy Father which seeth in secret shall reward thee openly.

Matthew 6:6

16

The Peace of Meditation

So we may know God better
And feel His quiet power,
Let us daily keep in silence
A MEDITATION HOUR —
For to understand God's greatness
And to use His gifts each day
The soul must learn to meet Him
In a meditative way,
For our Father tells His children
That if they would know His will
They must seek Him in the silence
When all is calm and still...
For nature's greatest forces
Are found in quiet things
Like softly falling snowflakes
Drifting down on angels' wings,
Or petals dropping soundlessly
From a lovely full-blown rose,
So God comes closest to us
When our souls are in repose...
So let us plan with prayerful care
To always allocate
A certain portion of each day
To be still and meditate...
For when everything is quiet
And we're lost in meditation,
Our soul is then preparing
For a deeper dedication
That will make it wholly possible
To quietly endure
The violent world around us —
For in God we are secure.

The Way to Love and Peace

There is no thinking person
Who can stand untouched today
And view the world around us
Slowly drifting to decay
Without feeling deep within them
A silent, unnamed dread
As they contemplate the future
That lies frighteningly ahead...
And as the "CLOUDS OF CHAOS"
Gather in man's muddled mind,
And he searches for the answer
He ALONE can never find,
Let us recognize we're facing
Problems man has never solved,
And with all our daily efforts
Life grows more and more involved,
But our future will seem brighter
And we'll meet with less resistance
If we call upon our Father
And seek Divine Assistance...
For the spirit can unravel
Many tangled, knotted threads
That defy the skill and power
Of the world's best hands and heads,
And our plans for growth and progress,
Of which we all have dreamed,
Cannot survive materially
Unless OUR SPIRITS are redeemed...
For only when the mind of man
Is united with the soul
Can LOVE and PEACE combine to make
Our lives complete and whole.

...the fruit of the Spirit is love ...peace....
Galatians 5:22

18

"In Him We Live, and Move, and Have Our Being"

We walk in a world that is strange and unknown
And in the midst of the crowd we still feel alone,
We question our purpose, our part and our place
In this vast land of mystery suspended in space,
We probe and explore and try hard to explain
The tumult of thoughts that our minds entertain...
But all of our probings and complex explanations
Of man's inner feelings and fears and frustrations
Still leave us engulfed in the "MYSTERY of LIFE"
With all of its struggles and suffering and strife,
Unable to fathom what tomorrow will bring —
But there is one truth to which we can cling,
For while LIFE'S a MYSTERY man can't understand
The "GREAT GIVER of LIFE" is holding our hand
And safe in HIS care there is no need for seeing
For "IN HIM WE LIVE and MOVE and HAVE OUR BEING."

**For in him we live, and move, and have our being;
as certain also of your own poets have said,
For we are also his offspring.**

Acts 17:28

19

For I am persuaded,
that neither death, nor life, nor angels,
nor principalities, nor powers,
nor things present, nor things to come,
Nor height, nor depth, nor any other creature,
shall be able to separate us from the love of God,
which is in Christ Jesus our Lord.

Romans 8:38,39

What More Can You Ask

God's love endureth forever—
What a wonderful thing to know
When the tides of life run against you
And your spirit is downcast and low...

God's kindness is ever around you,
Always ready to freely impart
Strength to your faltering spirit,
Cheer to your lonely heart...

God's presence is ever beside you,
As near as the reach of your hand,
You have but to tell Him your troubles,
There is nothing He won't understand...

And knowing God's love is unfailing,
And His mercy unending and great,
You have but to trust in His promise—
"God comes not too soon or too late"...

So wait with a heart that is patient
For the goodness of God to prevail—
For never do prayers go unanswered,
And His mercy and love never fail.

And he arose, and came to his father.
But when he was yet a great way off,
his father saw him, and had compassion, and ran,
and fell on his neck, and kissed him.

Luke 15:20

The Prodigal Son

With riches and youth to squander
The pleasure-bent "PRODIGAL SON"
Left the house of his Father
In search of adventure and fun —
And in reckless and riotous living
He wasted his youth and his gold,
And stripped of his earthly possessions
He was hungry and friendless and cold —
And thus he returned to his Father
Who met him with arms open wide
And cried, "My Son, you are welcome
And a banquet awaits you inside"...
Now this story is told to remind us
Not so much of the wandering Son
But THE UNCHANGING LOVE OF THE FATHER
Who gladly forgave all he'd done —
And the message contained in this story
Is a powerful, wonderful one,
For it shows us OUR FATHER IN HEAVEN
Waits to welcome each PRODIGAL SON —
And whatever have been our transgressions,
God is waiting to welcome us back
And restore us our place in His Kingdom
And give us the joy that we lack...
So wander no longer in darkness,
Let not your return be delayed,
For the door to God is wide open
To welcome "the sheep that have strayed."

God Gave Man the Earth to Enjoy — Not to Destroy

"The earth is the Lord's and the fullness thereof" —
He gave it to man as a Gift of His Love
So all men might live as He hoped that they would,
Sharing together all things that were good...
But man only destroyed "the good earth of God" —
He polluted the air and ravished the sod,
He cut down the forests with ruthless disdain,
And the earth's natural beauty he perverted for gain...
And all that God made and all that He meant
To bring man great blessings and a life of content
Have only made man a "giant of greed"
In a world where the password is "SEX, SIN and
    SPEED"...
And now in an age filled with violent dissent
Man finds he's imprisoned in his own discontent —
He has taken the earth that God placed in man's care
And built his own "hell" without being aware
That the future we face was fashioned by man
Who in ignorance resisted GOD'S BEAUTIFUL PLAN,
And what God created to be paradise
Became by man's lust and perversion and vice
A "caldron of chaos" in a "fog of pollution"
To which man can find no cure or solution —
How far man will go to complete his destruction
Is beyond a computer's robot deduction.

**The earth is the Lord's, and the fulness thereof;
the world, and they that dwell therein.**

Psalms 24:1

He Loves You!

It's amazing and incredible,
But it's as true as it can be,
God loves and understands us all
And that means YOU and ME —
His grace is all sufficient
For both the YOUNG and OLD,
For the lonely and the timid,
For the brash and for the bold —
His love knows no exceptions,
So never feel excluded,
No matter WHO or WHAT you are
Your name has been included —
And no matter what your past has been,
Trust God to understand,
And no matter what your problem is
Just place it in His Hand —
For in all of our UNLOVELINESS
This GREAT GOD LOVES US STILL,
He loved us since the world began
And what's more, HE ALWAYS WILL!

**...I have loved thee with an everlasting love:
therefore with lovingkindness have I drawn thee.**

Jeremiah 31:3

Give Me the Contentment of Acceptance

In the deep, dark hours of my distress
My unworthy life seems a "miserable mess" —
Handicapped, limited, with my strength decreasing
The demands on my time keep forever increasing
And I pray for the flair and the force of youth
So I can keep spreading GOD'S LIGHT and HIS TRUTH
For my heart's happy hope and my dearest desire
Is to continue to serve YOU with fervor and fire
But I no longer have strength to dramatically do
The spectacular things I loved doing for YOU
Forgetting entirely that all YOU required
Was not a "servant" the world admired
But a humbled heart and a sanctified soul
Whose only mission and purpose and goal
Was to be content with whatever GOD sends
And to know that to please YOU really depends
Not on continued and mounting success
But in learning how to become "LESS and LESS"
And to realize that we serve GOD best
When our one desire and only request
Is not to succumb to worldly acclaim
But honoring ourselves in YOUR HOLY NAME —
So let me say "NO" to all flattery and praise
And quietly spend the rest of my days
Far from the greed and the speed of man
Who has so distorted GOD'S simple life plan...
And let me be great in the eyes of THE LORD
For that is the richest, most priceless reward.

...I have learned, in whatsoever state I am,
therewith to be content.

Philippians 4:11

Nothing on Earth Is Forever Yours —
Only the Love of the Lord Endures!

Everything in life is passing
     and whatever we possess
Cannot endure forever
     but ends in nothingness,
For there are no safety boxes
     nor vaults that can contain
The possessions we collected
     and desire to retain...
So all that man acquires,
     be it power, fame or jewels,
Is but limited and earthly,
     only "treasure made for fools"...
For only in GOD'S KINGDOM
     can man find enduring treasure,
Priceless gifts of love and beauty —
     more than mortal man can measure,
And the "riches" he accumulates
     he can keep and part with never,
For only in GOD'S KINGDOM
     do our treasures last FOREVER...
So use the word FOREVER
     with sanctity and love,
For NOTHING IS FOREVER
     BUT THE LOVE OF GOD ABOVE!

Keep yourselves in the love of God,
looking for the mercy of our Lord Jesus Christ
unto eternal life.

Jude 21

...Whosoever will come after me,
let him deny himself,
and take up his cross,
and follow me.

Mark 8:34

28

Is the Cross You Wear
Too Heavy to Bear?

Complainingly I told myself,
    "this cross is too heavy to wear"
And I wondered discontentedly
    why God gave it to me to bear.
And I looked with envy at others
    whose crosses seemed lighter than mine
And wished that I could change my cross
    for one of a lighter design —
And then, in a dream, I beheld the cross
    I impulsively wanted to wear,
It was fashioned of pearls and diamonds
    and gems that were precious and rare.
And when I hung it around my neck
    the weight of the jewels and the gold
Was much too heavy and cumbersome
    for my small, slender neck to hold —
So I tossed it aside and before my eyes
    was a cross of rose-red flowers
And I said with delight as I put it on,
    "this cross I can wear for hours" —
For it was so dainty and fragile,
    so lovely and light and thin,
But I had forgotten about the thorns
    that started to pierce my skin —
And then in my dream I saw "my cross,"
    rugged and old and plain,
That clumsy old cross I had looked upon
    with discontented disdain —
And at last I knew that God had made
    this "special cross for me,"
For God in His great wisdom knew
    what I before could not see,
That often the loveliest crosses
    are the heaviest crosses to bear,
For only God is wise enough
    to choose the cross we can wear —
So never complain about YOUR CROSS,
    for your cross has been blest,
God made it JUST FOR YOU to wear
    and remember, GOD KNOWS BEST!

So Many Reasons
to Love the Lord

Thank You, God, for little things
     that come unexpectedly
To brighten up a dreary day
     that dawned so dismally —
Thank You, God, for sending
     a happy thought my way
To blot out my depression
     on a disappointing day —
Thank You, God, for brushing
     the "dark clouds" from my mind
And leaving only "sunshine"
     and joy of heart behind...
Oh, God, the list is endless
     of things to thank You for
But I take them all for granted
     and unconsciously ignore
That EVERYTHING I THINK or DO,
     each movement that I make,
Each measured rhythmic heartbeat,
     each breath of life I take
Is something You have given me
     for which there is no way
For me in all my "smallness"
     to in any way repay.

**Every good gift and every perfect gift
is from above, and cometh down from the
Father of lights, with whom is no variableness,
neither shadow of turning.**

James 1:17

God Is Never Beyond Our Reach

No one ever sought the Father
And found HE was not THERE,
And no burden is too heavy
To be lightened by a prayer,
No problem is too intricate
And no sorrow that we face
Is too deep and devastating
To be softened by His grace,
No trials and tribulations
Are beyond what we can bear
If we share them with OUR FATHER
As we talk to HIM in prayer —
And men of every color,
Every race and every creed
Have but to seek the Father
In their deepest hour of need —
God asks for no credentials,
He accepts us with our flaws,
He is kind and understanding
And He welcomes us because
We are His erring children
And He loves us everyone,
And He freely and completely
Forgives all that we have done,
Asking only if we're ready
To follow WHERE HE LEADS —
Content that in His wisdom
He will answer all our needs.

Ask, and it shall be given you;
seek, and ye shall find;
knock, and it shall be opened unto you.

Matthew 7:7

Listen in Silence
if You Would Hear

Silently the green leaves grow
In silence falls the soft, white snow
Silently the flowers bloom
In silence sunshine fills a room
Silently bright stars appear
In silence velvet night draws near...
And silently GOD enters in
To free a troubled heart from sin
For GOD works silently in lives
For nothing spiritual survives
Amid the din of a noisy street
Where raucous crowds with hurrying feet
And "blinded eyes" and "deafened ear"
Are never privileged to hear
The message GOD wants to impart
To every troubled, weary heart
For only in a QUIET PLACE
Can man behold GOD FACE to FACE!

Be still, and know that I am God.

Psalms 46:10

Talk It Over With God

You're worried and troubled
    about everything,
Wondering and fearing
    what tomorrow will bring —
You long to tell someone
    for you feel so alone,
But your friends are all burdened
    with cares of their own —
There is only one place
    and only ONE FRIEND
Who is never too busy
    and you can always depend
That HE will be waiting
    with arms open wide
To hear all your troubles
    that you came to confide —
For the heavenly Father
    will always be there
When you seek HIM and find HIM
    at THE ALTAR of PRAYER.

**And all things, whatsoever ye shall ask
in prayer, believing, ye shall receive.**

Matthew 21:22

Trust in the Lord, and do good;
so shalt thou dwell in the land,
and verily thou shalt be fed.

Delight thyself also in the Lord;
and he shall give thee the desires of thine heart.

Commit thy way unto the Lord;
trust also in him;
and he shall bring it to pass.

Rest in the Lord,
and wait patiently for him.

Psalms: 37:3-5, 7

Your Problems!
My Problems!
Our Problems!

Whatever your problem,
Whatever your cross,
Whatever your burden,
Whatever your loss,
You've got to believe me
You are not alone,
For all of the troubles
And trials you have known
Are faced at this minute
By others like you
Who also cry out,
"Oh, GOD, what shall I do?"...
I read many letters
From far countries and places,
I see eyes of sadness
In hundreds of faces,
And I, too, feel "the thorns
And the bruises of life"
And "the great stabbing pain
Of sorrow's sharp knife,"
But I know in my heart
This will, too, pass away...
And so as you read this
I implore you today
Find comfort in knowing
This is GOD'S way of saying
"COME UNTO ME"
And never cease praying,
For whatever your problem
Or whatever your sorrow
GOD holds "THE KEY"
To a BRIGHTER TOMORROW!

Are You Dissatisfied
With Yourself?

We are often discontented
      and much dissatisfied
That our wish for recognition
      has not been gratified...
We feel that we've been cheated
      in beauty, charm, and brains
And we think of all our "losses"
      and forget all about our "gains"...
And dwelling on the things we lack
      we grow miserable inside,
Brooding on our "deficits"
      that are born of selfish pride...
We begin to harbor hatred
      and envy fills our heart
That we do not possess the things
      that make others "seem so smart"...
And in our condemnation
      of the traits that we possess
We magnify our painful plight
      and sink deeper in distress...
Oh, Lord, forgive our foolishness,
      our vanity, and pride
As we strive to please the eye of man
      and not GOD who sees "INSIDE"...
And little do we realize
      how contented we would be
If we knew that we were "BEAUTIFUL"
      when our hearts are touched by THEE!

**...man looks on the outward appearance,
but the Lord looks on the heart.**

1 Samuel 16:7   RSV

Prayers Can't Be Answered
Unless They Are Prayed

Life without purpose is barren indeed —
There can't be a harvest unless you plant seed,
There can't be attainment unless there's a goal,
And man's but a robot unless there's a soul...
If we send no ships out, no ships will come in,
And unless there's a contest, nobody can win...
For games can't be won unless they are played,
And PRAYERS can't be ANSWERED unless they are PRAYED...
So whatever is wrong with your life today,
You'll find a solution if you kneel down and pray
Not just for pleasure, enjoyment and health,
Not just for honors and prestige and wealth...
But PRAY FOR A PURPOSE to MAKE LIFE WORTH LIVING,
And PRAY FOR THE JOY of UNSELFISH GIVING,
For GREAT IS YOUR GLADNESS and RICH YOUR REWARD
When you make your LIFE'S PURPOSE the choice of the Lord.

But seek ye first the kingdom of God,
and his righteousness;
and all these things shall be added unto you.

Matthew 6:33

For all things are for your sakes,
that the abundant grace might through
the thanksgiving of many redound
to the glory of God.

For our light affliction, which is
but for a moment, worketh for us a far more
exceeding and eternal weight of glory.

2 Corinthians 4:15, 17

Trouble Is a Stepping-Stone
to Growth

Trouble is something no one can escape,
Everyone has it in some form or shape —
Some people hide it way down deep inside,
Some people bear it with gallant-like pride,
Some people worry and complain of their lot,
Some people covet what they haven't got,
While others rebel and become bitter and old
With hopes that are dead and hearts that are cold...
But the wise man accepts whatever God sends,
Willing to yield like a storm-tossed tree bends,
Knowing that God never makes a mistake,
So whatever He sends they are willing to take —
For trouble is part and parcel of life
And no man can grow without trouble and strife,
And the steep hills ahead and high mountain peaks
Afford man at last the peace that he seeks —
So blest are the people who learn to accept
The trouble men try to escape and reject,
For in OUR ACCEPTANCE
         we're given great grace
And courage and faith and the strength to face
The daily troubles that come to us all
So we may learn to stand "straight and tall" —
For the grandeur of life is born of defeat
For in overcoming we make life complete.

Why art thou cast down, O my soul?
and why art thou disquieted within me?
hope thou in God:
for I shall yet praise him, who is the health
of my countenance, and my God.

Psalms 42:11

The Seasons of the Soul

Why am I cast down
    and despondently sad
When I long to be happy
    and joyous and glad?
Why is my heart heavy
    with unfathomable weight
As I try to escape
    this soul-saddened state?
I ask myself often —
    "What makes life this way,
Why is the song silenced
    in the heart that was gay?"
And then with God's help
    it all becomes clear,
The SOUL has its SEASONS
    just the same as the year —
I too must pass through
    life's autumn of dying,
A desolate period
    of heart-hurt and crying,
Followed by winter
    in whose frostbitten hand
My heart is as frozen
    as the snow-covered land —
Yes, man too must pass
    through the seasons God sends,
Content in the knowledge
    that everything ends,
And oh what a blessing
    to know there are reasons
And to find that our soul
    must, too, have its seasons —
BOUNTEOUS SEASONS
    and BARREN ONES, too,
Times for rejoicing
    and times to be blue,
But meeting these seasons
    of dark desolation
With strength that is born
    of anticipation
That comes from knowing
    that "autumn-time sadness"
Will surely be followed
    by a "Springtime of Gladness."

When Trouble Comes and Things Go Wrong!

Let us go quietly to God
      when troubles come to us,
Let us never stop to whimper
      or complain and fret and fuss,
Let us hide "our thorns" in "roses"
      and our sighs in "golden song"
And "our crosses" in a "crown of smiles"
      whenever things go wrong...
For no one can really help us
      as our troubles we bemoan,
For COMFORT, HELP and INNER PEACE
      MUST COME FROM GOD ALONE...
So do not tell your neighbor,
      your companion or your friend
In the hope that they can help you
      bring your troubles to an end...
For they, too, have their problems,
      they are burdened just like you,
So TAKE YOUR CROSS TO JESUS
      and HE WILL SEE YOU THROUGH...
And waste no time in crying
      on the shoulder of a friend
But go directly to the Lord
      for on Him you can depend...
For there's absolutely NOTHING
      that His mighty hand can't do
And He never is too busy
      to help and comfort you.

Come unto me, all ye that labour and are heavy laden, and I will give you rest.

Matthew 11:28

42

"This Too Will Pass Away"

If I can endure for this minute
Whatever is happening to me,
No matter how heavy my heart is
Or how "dark" the moment may be —
If I can remain calm and quiet
With all my world crashing about me,
Secure in the knowledge God loves me
When everyone else seems to doubt me —
If I can but keep on believing
What I know in my heart to be true,
That "darkness will fade with the morning"
And that THIS WILL PASS AWAY, TOO —
Then nothing in life can defeat me
For as long as this knowledge remains
I can suffer whatever is happening
For I know God will break "all the chains"
That are binding me tight in "THE DARKNESS"
And trying to fill me with fear —
For there is NO NIGHT WITHOUT DAWNING
And I know that "MY MORNING" is near.

...weeping may endure for a night,
but joy cometh in the morning.

Psalms 30:5

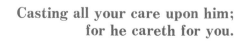

**Casting all your care upon him;
for he careth for you.**

1 Peter 5:7

Burdens Are Things
God Turns Into Wings

"Oh for the wings of a bird," we cry,
To carry us off to an untroubled sky
Where we can dwell untouched by care
And always be free as a bird in the air —
But there is a legend that's very old,
Not often heard and seldom told,
That once all birds were wingless, too,
Unable to soar through the skies of blue —
For, while their plumage was beautifully bright
And their chirping songs were liltingly light,
They, too, were powerless to fly
Until one day when the Lord came by
And laid at the feet of the singing birds
Gossamer wings as He spoke these words:
"Come take these burdens, so heavy now,
But if you bear them you'll learn somehow
That as you wear them they'll grow light
And soon you can lift yourself into flight" —
So folding the wings beneath their hearts,
And after endless failures and starts,
They lifted themselves and found with delight
The wings that were heavy had grown so light —
So let us, too, listen to God's wise words,
For we are much like the "wingless birds,"
And if we would shoulder our daily trials
And learn to wear them with sunny smiles
We'd find they were wings that God had sent
To lift us above our heart's discontent —
For THE WINGS that LIFT us out of despair
Are made by God from the weight of care,
So whenever you cry for "the wings of a bird"
Remember this little legend you've heard
And let God give you a heart that sings
As He turns your burdens to "silver wings."

Peoples' Problems

EVERYONE has problems
     in this restless world of care,
EVERYONE grows weary
     with the "cross they have to bear,"
EVERYONE is troubled
     and "their skies are overcast"
As they try to face the future
     while still dwelling in the past...
But the people with their problems
     only "listen with one ear"
For people only listen
     to the things they want to hear
And they only hear the kind of things
     they are able to believe
And the ANSWERS that are God's to give
     they're not ready to receive,
So while the PEOPLES' PROBLEMS
     keep growing every day
And man vainly tries to solve them
     in his own self-willful way...
God seeks to help and watches,
     waiting always patiently
To help them solve their problems
     whatever they may be —
So may the people of all nations
     at last become aware
That God will solve the PEOPLES' PROBLEMS
     through FAITH and HOPE and PRAYER!

**Call unto me, and I will answer thee,
and shew thee great and mighty things, which thou
knowest not.**

Jeremiah 33:3

Life's Bitterest Disappointments
Are God's Sweetest Appointments

Out of life's misery born of man's sins
A fuller, richer life begins,
For when we are helpless with no place to go
And our hearts are heavy and our spirits are low,
If we place, our poor, broken lives in GOD'S HANDS
And surrender completely to HIS WILL and DEMANDS,
The "darkness lifts" and the "sun shines through"
And by HIS TOUCH we are "born anew"...
So praise GOD for trouble that "cuts like a knife"
And disappointments that shatter your life,
For with PATIENCE to WAIT and FAITH to ENDURE
Your life will be blessed and your future secure,
For GOD is but testing your FAITH and your LOVE
Before HE "APPOINTS YOU" to rise far above
All the small things that so sorely distress you,
For GOD'S only intention is to strengthen and bless you.

Wherefore let them that suffer
according to the will of God
commit the keeping of their souls to him
in well doing,
as unto a faithful Creator.

1 Peter 4:19

It Takes the Bitter and the Sweet to Make a Life Full and Complete

Life is a mixture
      of sunshine and rain,
Laughter and teardrops,
      pleasure and pain —
Low tides and high tides,
      mountains and plains.
Triumphs, defeats
      and losses and gains —
But ALWAYS in ALL WAYS
      God's guiding and leading
And He alone knows
      the things we're most needing —
And when He sends sorrow
      or some dreaded affliction.
Be assured that it comes
      with God's kind benediction —
And if we accept it
      as a GIFT OF HIS LOVE.
We'll be showered with blessings
      from OUR FATHER ABOVE.

**For as many as are led by the Spirit of God,
they are the sons of God.
And we know that all things work together for good
to them that love God,
to them who are the called according to his
purpose.**

Romans 8:14, 28

Why Am I Complaining?

My cross is not too heavy,
My road is not too rough
Because God walks beside me
And to know this is enough...
And though I get so lonely
I know I'm not alone
For the Lord God is my Father
And He loves me as His own...
So though I'm tired and weary
And I wish my race were run
God will only terminate it
When my work on earth is done...
So let me stop complaining
About my "LOAD of CARE"
For God will always lighten it
When it gets too much to bear...
And if He does not ease my load
He will give me strength to bear it
For God in love and mercy
Is always near to share it.

When thou passest through the waters,
I will be with thee;
and through the rivers,
they shall not overflow thee:
when thou walkest through the fire,
thou shalt not be burned.

Isaiah 43:2

Adversity Can Distress Us
or Bless Us

The way we use adversity
      is strictly our own choice.
For in God's Hands adversity
      can make the heart rejoice —
For everything God sends to us,
      no matter in what form,
Is sent with plan and purpose
      for by the fierceness of a storm
The atmosphere is changed and cleared
      and the earth is washed and clean
And the "high winds of adversity"
      can make restless souls serene —
And while it's very difficult
      for mankind to understand
God's intentions and His purpose
      and the workings of His Hand.
If we observe the miracles
      that happen every day
We cannot help but be convinced
      that in His wondrous way
God makes what seemed unbearable
      and painful and distressing.
Easily acceptable
      when we view it as a blessing.

**For our light affliction,
which is but for a moment,
worketh for us a far more exceeding
and eternal weight of glory.**

2 Corinthians 4:17

How Great the Yield
From a Fertile Field

The farmer ploughs through the fields of green
And the blade of the plough is sharp and keen,
But the seed must be sown to bring forth grain,
For nothing is born without suffering and pain —
And God never ploughs in the soul of man
Without intention and purpose and plan,
So whenever you feel the plough's sharp blade
Let not your heart be sorely afraid
For, like the farmer, God chooses a field
From which He expects an excellent yield —
So rejoice though your heart is broken in two,
God seeks to bring forth a rich harvest in you.

He that goeth forth and weepeth,
bearing precious seed,
shall doubtless come again with rejoicing,
bringing his sheaves with him.

Psalms 126:6

Let not your heart be troubled:
ye believe in God, believe also in me.

Peace I leave with you,
my peace I give unto you:
not as the world giveth, give I unto you.
Let not your heart be troubled,
neither let it be afraid.

John 14:1, 27

Let Not Your Heart Be Troubled

Whenever I am troubled
        and lost in deep despair
I bundle all my troubles up
        and go to God in prayer...
I tell Him I am heartsick
        and lost and lonely, too,
That my mind is deeply burdened
        and I don't know what to do...
But I know He stilled the tempest
        and calmed the angry sea
And I humbly ask if in His love
        He'll do the same for me...
And then I just keep quiet
        and think only thoughts of Peace
And if I abide in stillness
        my "restless murmurings" cease.

Dark Shadows Fall
in the Lives of Us All

Sickness and sorrow
     come to us all,
But through it we grow
     and learn to "stand tall" —
For trouble is "part
     and parcel of life"
And no man can grow
     without struggle and strife,
And the more we endure
     with patience and grace
The stronger we grow
     and the more we can face —
And the more we can face,
     the greater our love,
And with love in our hearts
     we are more conscious of
The pain and the sorrow
     in lives everywhere,
So it is through trouble
     that we learn how to share.

...I will be with him in trouble;
I will deliver him, and honour him.

Psalms 91:15

Blessings Come
in Many Guises

When troubles come
       and things go wrong.
And days are cheerless
       and nights are long.
We find it so easy
       to give in to despair
By magnifying
       the burdens we bear —
We add to our worries
       by refusing to try
To look for "the rainbow"
       in an overcast sky —
And the blessing God sent
       in a "darkened disguise"
Our troubled hearts
       fail to recognize,
Not knowing God sent it
       not to distress us
But to strengthen our faith
       and redeem us and bless us.

As for God, his way is perfect.

Psalms 18:30

If ye then, being evil,
know how to give good
gifts unto your children,
how much more shall your Father
which is in heaven give good
things to them that ask him?

Matthew 7:11

Beyond Our Asking

More than hearts can imagine
        or minds comprehend,
God's bountiful gifts
        are ours without end —
We ask for a cupful
        when the vast sea is ours,
We pick a small rosebud
        from a garden of flowers,
We reach for a sunbeam
        but the sun still abides,
We draw one short breath
        but there's air on all sides —
Whatever we ask for
        falls short of God's giving
For His Greatness exceeds
        every facet of living,
And always God's ready
        and eager and willing
To pour out His mercy
        completely fulfilling
All of man's needs
        for peace, joy and rest
For God gives His children
        Whatever Is Best —
Just give Him a chance
        to open His Treasures
And He'll fill your life
        with unfathomable pleasures,
Pleasures that never
        grow worn out and faded
And leave us depleted,
        disillusioned and jaded —
For God has a "storehouse"
        just filled to the brim
With all that man needs
        if we'll only ask Him

... and behold a ladder set up on the earth, and the top of it reached to heaven: and behold the angels of God ascending and descending on it. And, behold, the Lord stood above it, and said, I am the Lord God....I am with thee, and will keep thee in all places whither thou goest.

Genesis 28:12, 13, 15

Prayers Are
the Stairs to God

Prayers are the stairs
We must climb every day,
If we would reach God
There is no other way,
For we learn to know God
When we meet Him in prayer
And ask Him to lighten
Our burden of care —
So start in the morning
And, though the way's steep,
Climb ever upward
'Til your eyes close in sleep —
For prayers are the stairs
That lead to the Lord,
And to meet Him in prayer
Is the climber's reward.

He hath shewed thee, O man, what is good;
and what doth the Lord require of thee,
but to do justly, and to love mercy,
and to walk humbly with thy God?

Micah 6:8

He Asks So Little
and Gives So Much

WHAT MUST I DO
      to insure peace of mind?
Is the answer I'm seeking,
      too hard to find?
HOW CAN I KNOW
      what God wants me to be?
HOW CAN I TELL
      what's expected of me?
WHERE CAN I GO
      for guidance and aid
To help me correct
      the errors I've made?
The answer is found
      in doing THREE THINGS
And great is the gladness
      that doing them brings...
"DO JUSTICE" — "LOVE KINDNESS" —
      "WALK HUMBLY WITH GOD" —
For with these THREE THINGS
      as your "rule and your rod"
All things worth having
      are yours to achieve
If you follow God's words
      and have FAITH to BELIEVE!

...Man shall not live by bread alone,
but by every word that
proceedeth out of the mouth of God.

Matthew 4:4

Thou preparest a table before me
in the presence of mine enemies.

Psalms 23:5

Man Cannot Live
by Bread Alone

He lived in a palace
      on a mountain of gold,
Surrounded by riches
      and wealth untold,
Priceless possessions
      and treasures of art,
But he died alone
      of a "HUNGRY HEART"!
For man cannot live
      by bread alone,
No matter what
      he may have or own...
For though he reaches
      his earthly goal
He'll waste away
      with a "starving soul"!
But he who eats
      of HOLY BREAD
Will always find
      his spirit fed,
And even the poorest
      of men can afford
To feast at the table
      prepared by the Lord.

Behold, I stand at the door, and knock:
if any man hear my voice, and open the door,
I will come in to him,
and will sup with him,
and he with me.

Revelation 3:20

Ask, and it shall be given you;
seek, and ye shall find;
knock, and it shall be opened unto you.

Matthew 7:7

No Prayer Goes Unheard

Often we pause and wonder
When we kneel down to pray —
Can God really hear
The prayers that we say...
But if we keep praying
And talking to HIM.
He'll brighten the soul
That was clouded and dim,
And as we continue
Our burden seems lighter,
Our sorrow is softened
And our outlook is brighter —
For though we feel helpless
And alone when we start,
Our prayer is the key
That opens the heart,
And as our heart opens
The dear Lord comes in
And the prayer that we felt
We could never begin
Is so easy to say
For the Lord understands
And gives us new strength
By the touch of His hands.

New Concepts and
Old Commandments

Living as we do today
     in a world of speed and greed,
We are restless and dissatisfied
     and we recognize a need
For something to alleviate
     our constant state of stress.
Something that will change dull days
     to hours of happiness,
Something new and different
     to excite our bored existence
Which we so foolishly attempt
     to change with rash resistance
By protesting we're entitled
     to the carnal-minded things,
Believing we'll be satisfied
     with the pleasure this life brings —
And in our discontentment
     we disregard restrictions
And decide to seek our happiness
     in delinquent derelictions —
We renounce our morals and ethics
     and reject all discipline,
Forgetting THE COMMANDMENTS
     governing now outmoded sin —
We are sure in our new freedom,
     with our lust and greed unleashed,
The "PINNACLE of PLEASURE"
     will certainly be reached —
But man cannot desecrate his soul
     or defy God's changeless laws
For the age-old TEN COMMANDMENTS
     STAND UNTOUCHED BY HUMAN
     FLAWS,
And until man comes to realize
     he must live and still obey
The COMMANDMENTS that God handed down
     way back in Moses' day,

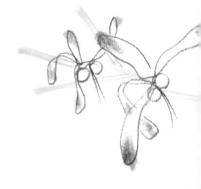

He will never find contentment
        and his search will be in vain
For what he thought was pleasure
        will return to him in pain —
For man with all his greatness,
        his knowledge and his skill,
Is still as helpless as a child
        and subject to God's will,
And there is nothing man can do
        to bring lasting joy and peace
Or curb his untamed passions
        or make his longings cease,
But the humble, full acknowledgment
        that there is no substitute
To bring forth a "HAPPY HARVEST"
        except the "SPIRIT'S FRUIT" —
For unless man's spirit is redeemed
        he will never, never find
Unblemished love and happiness
        and eternal peace of mind.

I am the Lord thy God....shewing mercy
unto thousands of them that love me,
and keep my commandments.

Exodus 20:2, 6

God, Grant Me the Glory
of "Thy Gift"

God, widen my vision so I may see
  the afflictions You have sent to me —
Not as a CROSS too heavy to wear
  that weights me down in gloomy despair —
Not as something to hate and despise
  but a GIFT of LOVE sent in disguise —
Something to draw me closer to You
  to teach me PATIENCE and
  FORBEARANCE, too —
Something to show me more clearly the way
  to SERVE You and LOVE You more
  every day —
Something PRICELESS and PRECIOUS and
  RARE
  that will keep me forever SAFE in Thy
  CARE
Aware of the SPIRITUAL STRENGTH that
  is mine
  if my selfish, small will is lost in Thine!

Most gladly therefore will I rather glory in my infirmities.

2 Corinthians 12:9

It is good for me that I have been afflicted.

Psalms 119:71

Not by Chance
nor Happenstance

Into our lives come many things
     to break the dull routine.
The things we had not planned on
     that happen unforeseen,
The unexpected little joys
     that are scattered on our way.
Success we did not count on
     or a rare, fulfilling day —
A catchy, lilting melody
     that makes us want to dance,
A nameless exaltation
     of enchantment and romance —
An unsought word of kindness,
     a compliment or two
That sets the eyes to gleaming
     like crystal drops of dew —
The unplanned sudden meeting
     that comes with sweet surprise
And lights the heart with happiness
     like a rainbow in the skies...
Now some folks call it fickle fate
And some folks call it chance,
While others just accept it
As a pleasant happenstance —
But no matter what you call it,
It didn't come without design,
For all our lives are fashioned
By the HAND THAT IS DIVINE —
And every happy happening
And every lucky break
Are little gifts from God above
That are ours to freely take.

**The steps of a good man
are ordered by the Lord.**

Psalms 37:23

I had fainted, unless I had believed
to see the goodness of the Lord in the land of the living.
Wait on the Lord:
be of good courage,
and he shall strengthen thine heart:
wait, I say, on the Lord.

Psalms 27:13, 14

The Soul of Man

Every man has a deep heart need
That cannot be filled with doctrine
      or creed,
For the soul of man knows nothing more
Than just that he is longing for
A haven that is safe and sure,
A fortress where he feels secure,
An island in this sea of strife,
Away from all the storms of life...
Oh, God of love, who sees us all,
YOU are SO GREAT! We are so small!
Hear man's universal prayer
Crying to you in despair –
"Save my soul and grant me peace,
Let my restless murmurings cease,
God of love, FORGIVE! FORGIVE!
Teach me how to TRULY LIVE...
Ask me not my race or creed
Just take me in MY HOUR of NEED
Let me feel You love me, too,
And that I AM A PART OF YOU."

For what shall it profit a man,
if he shall gain the whole world,
and lose his own soul?

Mark 8:36

Who Said, "God Is Dead"?

In this world of new concepts
       it has often been said —
Why heed the Commandments
       of a God who is dead,
Why follow His precepts
       that are old and outdated,
Restrictive and narrow
       and in no way related
To this modern-day world
       where the pace is so fast
It cannot be hampered
       by an old-fashioned past...
And yet this "DEAD GOD"
       still holds in His Hand
The star-studded sky,
       the sea and the land,
And with perfect precision
       the old earth keeps spinning
As flawlessly accurate
       as in "THE BEGINNING"...
So be not deceived
       by "the new pharisees"
Who boast man has only
       HIS OWN SELF TO PLEASE,
And who loudly proclaim
       any man is a fool
Who denies himself pleasure
       to follow God's rule...
But what can they offer
       that will last and endure
And make life's uncertainties
       safe and secure,
And what, though man gain
       the whole world and its pleasures,
If he loses his soul
       and "eternity's treasures"?

For we have not an high priest which cannot be touched
with the feeling of our infirmities;
but was in all points tempted like as we are,
yet without sin.

Let us therefore come boldly unto the throne of grace,
that we may obtain mercy,
and find grace to help in time of need.

Hebrews 4:15, 16

"He Was One of Us"

He was born as little children are
and lived as children do,
So remember that the Saviour
was once a child like you,
And remember that He lived on earth
in the midst of sinful men,
And the problems of the present
existed even then;
He was ridiculed and laughed at
in the same heartbreaking way
That we who fight for justice
are ridiculed today;
He was tempted...He was hungry...
He was lonely...He was sad...
There's no sorrowful experience
that the Saviour has not had;
And in the end He was betrayed
and even crucified,
For He was truly "One Of Us" —
He lived on earth and died;
So do not heed the skeptics
who are often heard to say:
"What Does God Up In Heaven
Know Of Things We Face Today"...
For, our Father up in heaven
is very much aware
Of our failures and shortcomings
and the burdens that we bear;
So whenever you are troubled
put your problems in God's Hand
For He has faced all problems
and He Will Understand.

"I Am the Way, the Truth, and the Life"

I AM THE WAY
  so just follow ME
Though the way be rough
  and you cannot see...

I AM THE TRUTH
  which all men seek
So heed not "false prophets"
  nor the words that they speak...

I AM THE LIFE
  and I hold the key
That opens the door
  to ETERNITY...

And in this dark world
  I AM THE LIGHT
TO THE PROMISED LAND
  WHERE THERE IS NO NIGHT!

I am the way, the truth, and the life.
I am the light of the world.

John 14:6; 8:12

On the Wings of Prayer

Just close your eyes and open your heart
And feel your worries and cares depart,
Just yield yourself to the Father above
And let Him hold you secure in His love —
For life on earth grows more involved
With endless problems that can't be solved —
But God only asks us to do our best,
Then He will "take over" and finish the rest —
So when you are tired, discouraged and blue,
There's always one door that is open to you —
And that is the door to "The House of Prayer"
And you'll find God waiting to meet you there,
And "The House of Prayer" is no farther away
Than the quiet spot where you kneel and pray —
For the heart is a temple when God is there
As we place ourselves in His loving care,
And He hears every prayer and answers each one
When we pray in His name "Thy Will Be Done" —
And the burdens that seemed too heavy to bear
Are lifted away on "The Wings of Prayer."

**Blessed is the man that heareth me,
watching daily at my gates.**

Proverbs 8:34

And this is the confidence that we have in him,
that, if we ask any thing according to his will, he heareth us.

1 John 5:14

Not What You Want
but What God Wills

Do you want WHAT YOU WANT when you
      want it...
Do you pray and expect a reply,
And when it's not instantly answered
Do you feel that God passed you by?
Well, prayers that are prayed in this manner
Are really not prayers at all
For you can't go to God in a hurry
And expect Him to answer your call...
For prayers are not meant for obtaining
What we selfishly wish to acquire,
For God in His wisdom refuses
The things that we wrongly desire...
And don't pray for freedom from trouble
Or ask that life's trials pass you by.
Instead, pray for strength and for courage
To meet life's "dark hours" and not cry
That God was not there when you called Him
And He turned a deaf ear to your prayer
And just when you needed Him most of all
He left you alone in despair...
WAKE UP! You are missing completely
The reason and purpose of prayer,
Which is really to keep us contented
That God holds us safe in His care...
And God only answers our pleadings
When He knows that our wants fill a need
And whenever "OUR WILL" becomes
      "HIS WILL"
There is NO PRAYER THAT GOD DOES
      NOT HEED!

Behold, I stand at the door, and knock:
if any man hear my voice, and open the door,
I will come in to him, and will sup with him,
and he with me.

Revelation 3:20

Where Can We Find Him?

Where can we find THE HOLY ONE?
Where can we see HIS ONLY SON?
The Wise Men asked, and we're asking still,
WHERE CAN WE FIND THIS MAN OF GOOD WILL?
Is He far away in some distant place,
Ruling unseen from His throne of grace?
Is there nothing on earth that man can see
To give him proof of ETERNITY?
It's true we have never looked on His face,
But His likeness shines forth from every place,
In everything both great and small
We see THE HAND OF GOD IN ALL,
And every day, somewhere, someplace,
We see THE LIKENESS OF HIS FACE...
For who can watch a new day's birth
Or touch the warm, life-giving earth,
Or feel the softness of the breeze
Or look at skies through lacy trees
And say they've never seen His face
Or looked upon His throne of grace...
And man's search for God will end and begin
When he opens his heart to let Christ in.

"What Has Been Is What Will Be ... and There Is Nothing New Under the Sun."

Today my soul is reaching out
For SOMETHING that's UNKNOWN,
I cannot grasp or fathom it
For it's known to God alone —
I cannot hold or harness it
Or put it into form,
For it's as uncontrollable
As the wind before the storm —
I know not WHERE it came from
Or WHITHER it will go,
For it's as inexplicable
As the restless winds that blow —
And like the wind it too will pass
And leave nothing more behind
Than the "MEMORY of a MYSTERY"
That blew across my mind —
But like the wind it will return
To keep reminding me
That everything that has been
Is what again will be —
For there is nothing that is new
Beneath God's timeless sun,
And present, past and future
Are all molded into one —
And east and west and north and south
The same wind keeps on blowing,
While rivers run on endlessly
Yet the sea's not overflowing —
And the restless unknown longing
Of my searching soul won't cease
Until God comes in glory
And my soul at last finds peace.

**The thing that hath been,
it is that which shall be;
and that which is done is
that which shall be done:
and there is no new thing under the sun.**

Ecclesiastes 1:9

Thank You, God, for Everything

Thank you, God, for everything — the big things and the small,
For "every good gift comes from God" — the giver of them all —
And all too often we accept without any thanks or praise
The gifts God sends as blessings each day in many ways —
First, thank you for the little things that often come our way,
The things we take for granted but don't mention when we pray,
Then, thank you for the "Miracles" we are much too blind to see,
And give us new awareness of our many gifts from Thee,
And help us to remember that the Key to Life and Living
Is to make each prayer a Prayer of Thanks and every day Thanksgiving.

For of him, and through him, and to him,
are all things:
to whom be glory for ever.

Romans 11:36

...in every thing by prayer and supplication with thanksgiving
let your requests be made known unto God.
And the peace of God,
which passeth all understanding,
shall keep your hearts and minds
through Christ Jesus.

Philippians 4:6, 7

Every Day Is a Holiday
to Thank and Praise the Lord

Special poems for special seasons
        are meaningful indeed,
But DAILY INSPIRATION
        is still man's greatest need—
For day by day all through the year,
        not just on holidays,
Man should glorify the Lord
        in deeds and words of praise—
And when the heart is heavy
        and everything goes wrong,
May these "Daily Words for Daily Needs"
        be like a cheery song
Assuring you "HE LOVES YOU"
        and that "YOU NEVER WALK ALONE"—
For in God's all-wise wisdom
        your EVERY NEED IS KNOWN!

The Lord is my shepherd; I shall not want.
He maketh me to lie down in green pastures:
     he leadeth me beside the still waters.
He restoreth my soul:
     he leadeth me in the paths of righteousness for his name's sake.
Yea, though I walk through the valley of the shadow of death,
     I will fear no evil: for thou art with me;
     thy rod and thy staff they comfort me.
Thou preparest a table before me in the presence of mine enemies:
     thou anointest my head with oil;
     my cup runneth over.
Surely goodness and mercy shall follow me all the days of my life:
     and I will dwell in the house of the Lord for ever.

Psalms 23

Look on the Sunny Side

There are always two sides, the Good and the Bad,
The Dark and the Light, the Sad and the Glad —
But in looking back over the Good and the Bad
We're aware of the number of Good Things we've had —
And in counting our blessings we find when we're through
We've no reason at all to complain or be blue —
So thank God for Good things He has already done,
And be grateful to Him for the battles you've won,
And know that the same God who helped you before
Is ready and willing to help you once more —
Then with faith in your heart reach out for God's Hand
And accept what He sends, though you can't understand —
For Our Father in heaven always knows what is best,
And if you trust in His wisdom your life will be blest,
For always remember that whatever betide you,
You are never alone for God is beside you.

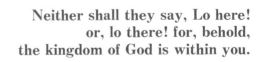

Neither shall they say, Lo here!
or, lo there! for, behold,
the kingdom of God is within you.

Luke 17:21

The Windows of Gold

There is a legend that has often been told
      Of the boy who searched for the Windows of Gold...
The beautiful windows he saw far away
      When he looked in the valley at sunrise each day...
And he yearned to go down to the valley below
      But he lived on a mountain that was covered with snow...
And he knew it would be a difficult trek,
      But that was a journey he wanted to make...
So he planned by day and he dreamed by night
      Of how he could reach The Great Shining Light...
And one golden morning when dawn broke through
      And the valley sparkled with diamonds of dew...
He started to climb down the mountainside
      With the Windows of Gold as his goal and his guide...
He traveled all day and, weary and worn,
      With bleeding feet and clothes that were torn...
He entered the peaceful valley town
      Just as the Golden Sun went down...
But he seemed to have lost his "Guiding Light" —
      The windows were dark that had once been bright...
And hungry and tired and lonely and cold
      He cried, "Won't You Show Me The Windows of Gold?"...
And a kind hand touched him and said, "Behold!
      High On The Mountain Are The Windows of Gold"
For the sun going down in a great golden ball
      Had burnished the windows of his cabin so small...
And the Kingdom of God with its Great Shining Light,
      Like the Golden Windows that shone so bright...
Is not a far distant place, somewhere,
      It's as close to you as a silent prayer...
And your search for God will end and begin
      When you look for Him and find Him WITHIN.

Let your light so shine before men,
that they may see your good works,
and glorify your Father which is in heaven.

Matthew 5:16

Brighten the Corner Where You Are

We cannot all be famous
      or be listed in "WHO's WHO,"
But every person great or small
      has important work to do,
For seldom do we realize
      the importance of small deeds
Or to what degree of greatness
      unnoticed kindness leads —
For it's not the big celebrity
      in a world of fame and praise,
But it's doing unpretentiously
      in undistinguished ways
The work that God assigned to us,
      unimportant as it seems,
That makes our task outstanding
      and brings reality to dreams —
So do not sit and idly wish
      for wider, new dimensions
Where you can put in practice
      your many "GOOD INTENTIONS" —
But at the spot God placed you
      begin at once to do
Little things to brighten up
      the lives surrounding you,
For if everybody brightened up
      the spot on which they're standing
By being more considerate
      and a little less demanding,
This dark old world would very soon
      eclipse the "Evening Star"
If everybody BRIGHTENED UP
      THE CORNER WHERE THEY ARE!

A merry heart doeth good like a medicine.

Proverbs 17:22

Keep thy heart with all diligence;
for out of it are the issues of life.

Proverbs 4:23

Be of Good Cheer —
There's Nothing to Fear!

Cheerful thoughts like sunbeams
Lighten up the "darkest fears"
For when the heart is happy
There's just no time for tears —
And when the face is smiling
It's impossible to frown
And when you are "high-spirited"
You cannot feel "low-down" —
For the nature of our attitude
Toward circumstantial things
Determines our acceptance
Of the problems that life brings.
And since fear and dread and worry
Cannot help in any way,
It's much healthier and happier
To be cheerful every day —
And if you'll only try it
You will find, without a doubt,
A cheerful attitude's something
No one should be without —
For when the heart is cheerful
It cannot be filled with fear.
And without fear the way ahead
Seems more distinct and clear —
And we realize there's nothing
We need ever face alone
For our HEAVENLY FATHER loves us
And our problems are His own.

Dearly beloved, avenge not yourselves,
but rather give place unto wrath:
for it is written, Vengeance is mine;
I will repay, saith the Lord.

Be not overcome of evil,
but overcome evil with good.

Romans 12:19, 21

Worry No More!
God Knows the Score!

Have you ever been caught
      in a web you didn't weave,
Involved in conditions
      that are hard to believe?
Have you felt you must speak
      and explain and deny
A story that's groundless
      or a small, whispered lie?
Have you ever heard rumors
      you would like to refute
Or some telltale gossip
      you would like to dispute?
Well, don't be upset
      for God knows the score
And with God as your judge
      you need worry no more,
For men may misjudge you
      but God's verdict is fair
For He looks deep inside
      and He is clearly aware
Of every small detail
      in your pattern of living
And always He's lenient
      and fair and forgiving —
And knowing that God
      is your judge and your jury
Frees you completely
      from man's falseness and fury,
And secure in this knowledge
      let your thoughts rise above
Man's small, shallow judgments
      that are so empty of
God's GOODNESS and GREATNESS
      in judging all men
And forget "ugly rumors"
      and be happy again.

This is the day which the Lord hath made;
we will rejoice and be glad in it.

Psalms 118:24

Yesterday ... Today ... and Tomorrow!

Yesterday's dead,
Tomorrow's unborn,
So there's nothing to fear
And nothing to mourn,
For all that is past
And all that has been
Can never return
To be lived once again —
And what lies ahead
Or the things that will be
Are still in GOD'S HANDS
So it is not up to me
To live in the future
That is God's great unknown,
For the past and the present
God claims for His own,
So all I need do
Is to live for TODAY
And trust God to show me
THE TRUTH and THE WAY —
For it's only the memory
Of things that have been
And expecting tomorrow
To bring trouble again
That fills my today,
Which God wants to bless,
With uncertain fears
And borrowed distress —
For all I need live for
Is this one little minute,
For life's HERE and NOW
And ETERNITY'S in it.

**With men it is impossible,
but not with God:
for with God
all things are possible.**

Mark 10:27

We Can't ...
but God Can!

Why things happen as they do
We do not always know,
And we cannot always fathom
Why our spirits sink so low...
We flounder in our dark distress,
We are wavering and unstable,
But when we're most inadequate
The Lord God's ALWAYS ABLE...
For though we are incapable,
God's powerful and great,
And there's no darkness of the mind
That God can't penetrate...
And all that is required of us
Whenever things go wrong
Is to trust in God implicitly
With a FAITH that's deep and strong,
And while He may not instantly
Unravel all the strands
Of the tangled thoughts that trouble us —
He completely understands...
And in His time, if we have FAITH,
He will gradually restore
The brightness to our spirit
That we've been longing for...
So remember, there's no cloud too dark
For God's light to penetrate
If we keep on believing
And have FAITH ENOUGH to WAIT!

Storms Bring Out
the Eagles but the
Little Birds Take Cover

When the "storms of life"
      gather darkly ahead,
I think of these wonderful words
      I once read
And I say to myself
      as "threatening clouds" hover
Don't "fold up your wings"
      and "run for cover"
But like the eagle
      "spread wide your wings"
And "soar far above"
      the troubles life brings,
For the eagle knows
      that the higher he flies
The more tranquil and brighter
      become the skies...
And there is nothing in life
      GOD ever asks us to bear
That we can't soar above
      "ON THE WINGS OF PRAYER,"
And in looking back over
      the "storm you passed through"
You'll find you gained strength
      and new courage, too,
For in facing "life's storms"
      with an EAGLE'S WINGS
You can fly far above
      earth's small, petty things.

...they that wait upon the Lord
shall renew their strength;
they shall mount up with wings as eagles....

Isaiah 40:31

Never Borrow Sorrow
From Tomorrow

Deal only with the present,
Never step into tomorrow,
For God asks us just to trust Him
And to never borrow sorrow —
For the future is not ours to know
And it may never be,
So let us live and give our best
And give it lavishly —
For to meet tomorrow's troubles
Before they are even ours
Is to anticipate the Saviour
And to doubt His all-wise powers —
So let us be content to solve
Our problems one by one,
Asking nothing of tomorrow
Except "THY WILL BE DONE."

But seek ye first the kingdom of God,
and his righteousness; and all
these things shall be added unto you.
Take therefore no thought for the morrow:
for the morrow shall take thought
for the things of itself.

Matthew 6:33, 34

Give Us Daily Awareness

On life's busy thoroughfares
We meet with angels unawares —
So, Father, make us kind and wise
So we may always recognize
The blessings that are ours to take,
The friendships that are ours to make
If we but open our heart's door wide
To let the sunshine of love inside.

**Let brotherly love continue. Be not forgetful
to entertain strangers: for thereby some have
entertained angels unawares.**

Hebrews 13:1, 2

The Gift of Friendship

Friendship is a priceless gift
That cannot be bought or sold,
But its value is far greater
Than a mountain made of gold—
For gold is cold and lifeless,
It can neither see nor hear,
And in the time of trouble
It is powerless to cheer—
It has no ears to listen,
No heart to understand,
It cannot bring you comfort
Or reach out a helping hand—
So when you ask God for a Gift,
Be thankful if He sends
Not diamonds, pearls or riches,
But the love of real true friends.

Two are better than one;
because they have a good reward for their labour.
...woe to him that is alone when he falleth;
for he hath not another to help him up.

Ecclesiastes 4:9, 10

Beloved, let us love one another:
for love is of God;
and every one that loveth is born of God,
and knoweth God.

1 John 4:7

Everybody Everywhere Needs Somebody Sometime

Everybody, everywhere,
    no matter what his station,
Has moments of deep loneliness
    and quiet desperation.
For this lost and lonely feeling
    is inherent in mankind —
It is just the SPIRIT SPEAKING
    as God tries again to find
An opening in the "worldly wall"
    man builds against God's touch,
For he feels so self-sufficient
    that he does not need God much.
So he vainly goes on struggling
    to find some explanation
For these disturbing, lonely moods
    of inner isolation . . .
But the answer keeps eluding him
    for in his selfish, finite mind
He does not even recognize
    that he cannot ever find
The reason for life's emptiness
    unless he learns to share
The problems and the burdens
    that surround him everywhere —
But when his eyes are opened
    and he looks with love at others
He begins to see not STRANGERS
    but understanding brothers. . .
So open up your hardened hearts
    and let God enter in —
HE only wants to help you
    a NEW LIFE TO BEGIN . . .
And EVERY DAY'S A GOOD DAY
    to lose yourself in others
And ANY TIME A GOOD TIME
    TO SEE MANKIND AS BROTHERS.
And this can only happen
    when you realize it's true
That EVERYONE NEEDS SOMEONE
    and that SOMEONE IS YOU!

A friend loveth at all times,
and a brother is born for adversity.

Proverbs 17:17

A Friend Is a Gift of God

Among the great and glorious gifts
      our heavenly Father sends
Is the GIFT of UNDERSTANDING
      that we find in loving friends,
For in this world of trouble
      that is filled with anxious care
Everybody needs a friend
      in whom they're free to share
The little secret heartaches
      that lay heavy on their mind,
Not just a mere acquaintance
      but someone who's "JUST OUR KIND" —
For, somehow, in the generous heart
      of loving, faithful friends
The good God in His charity
      and wisdom always sends
A sense of understanding
      and the power of perception
And mixes these fine qualities
      with kindness and affection
So when we need some sympathy
      or a friendly hand to touch,
Or an ear that listens tenderly
      and speaks words that mean so much,
We seek our true and trusted friend
      in the knowledge that we'll find
A heart that's sympathetic
      and an understanding mind...
And often just without a word
      there seems to be a union
Of thoughts and kindred feelings
      for GOD gives TRUE FRIENDS communion.

Unaware, We Pass "Him" By

On life's busy thoroughfares
We meet with ANGELS unawares—
But we are too busy to listen or hear,
Too busy to sense that God is near,
Too busy to stop and recognize
The grief that lies in another's eyes,
Too busy to offer to help or share,
Too busy to sympathize or care,
Too busy to do the GOOD THINGS we should.
Telling ourselves we would if we could . . .
But life is too swift and the pace is too great
And we dare not pause for we might be late
For our next appointment which means so much,
We are willing to brush off the Saviour's touch.
And we tell ourselves there will come a day
We will have more time to pause on our way . . .
But before we know it "life's sun has set"
And we've passed the Saviour but never met,
For hurrying along life's thoroughfare
We passed Him by and remained unaware
That within the VERY SIGHT OF OUR EYE,
UNNOTICED, THE SON OF GOD PASSED BY.

Then shall they also answer him, saying, Lord, when saw we thee an hungred, or athirst, or a stranger, or naked, or sick, or in prison, and did not minister unto thee?

Then shall he answer them, saying, Verily I say unto you, Inasmuch as ye did it not to one of the least of these, ye did it not to me.

Matthew 25:44, 45

Help Yourself
to Happiness

Everybody, everywhere
seeks happiness, it's true,
But finding it and keeping it
seems difficult to do,
Difficult because we think
that happiness is found
Only in the places where
wealth and fame abound—
And so we go on searching
in "palaces of pleasure"
Seeking recognition
and monetary treasure,
Unaware that happiness
is just a "state of mind"
Within the reach of everyone
who takes time to be kind—
For in making OTHERS HAPPY
we will be happy, too,
For the happiness you give away
returns to "shine on you."

Give, and it shall be given unto you;
good measure, pressed down, and shaken together,
and running over.

Luke 6:38

She openeth her mouth with wisdom;
and in her tongue is the law of kindness.
She looketh well to the ways of her household,
and eateth not the bread of idleness.
Her children arise up, and call her blessed;
her husband also, and he praiseth her.

Proverbs 31:26-28

A Mother's Love Is a Haven
in the Storms of Life

A MOTHER'S LOVE is like an island
    In life's ocean vast and wide,
A peaceful, quiet shelter
    From the restless, rising tide...

A MOTHER'S LOVE is like a fortress
    And we seek protection there
When the waves of tribulation
    Seem to drown us in despair...

A MOTHER'S LOVE'S a sanctuary
    Where our souls can find sweet rest
From the struggle and the tension
    Of life's fast and futile quest...

A MOTHER'S LOVE is like a tower
    Rising far above the crowd,
And her smile is like the sunshine
    Breaking through a threatening cloud...

A MOTHER'S LOVE is like a beacon
    Burning bright with FAITH and PRAYER,
And through the changing scenes of life
    We can find a HAVEN THERE...

For A MOTHER'S LOVE is fashioned
    After God's enduring love,
It is endless and unfailing
    Like the love of HIM above...

For God knew in HIS great wisdom
    That HE couldn't be EVERYWHERE
So HE put HIS LITTLE CHILDREN
    In a LOVING MOTHER'S CARE.

Peace on Earth,
Good Will Toward Men

As we have therefore opportunity,
let us do good unto all men....

Galatians 6:10

GOD placed the peace HE promised
    into the hands of man,
But man has never kept that peace
    since endless time began...
For man has never understood,
    either now or then,
That peace comes not through battles
    but "DOING GOOD UNTO ALL MEN"!
And when we meet with "strangers"
    on life's busy thoroughfares,
"Be not forgetful that thereby
    oft angels pass us unawares"...
And when we are at peace with GOD
    then only will we find
THE PEACE on EARTH HE promised
    and ETERNAL PEACE of MIND.

Thou wilt keep him in perfect peace,
whose mind is stayed on thee....

Isaiah 26:3

Peace Begins in the Home and the Heart

Peace is not something you fight for
With bombs and missiles that kill,
Nor can it be won in a "battle of words"
Man fashions by scheming and skill...
For men who are greedy and warlike,
Whose avarice for power cannot cease,
Can never contribute in helping
To bring this world nearer to peace...
For in seeking PEACE for ALL PEOPLE
There is only one place to begin
And that is in each HOME and HEART —
For the FORTRESS of PEACE is WITHIN!

Peace I leave with you,
my peace I give unto you:
not as the world giveth,
give I unto you.
Let not your heart be troubled,
neither let it be afraid.

John 14:27

What Is a Baby?

A baby is a GIFT OF LIFE
        born of "the wonder of love,"
A little bit of ETERNITY
        sent from THE FATHER ABOVE,
Giving a new dimension
        to the love between husband and wife
And putting an added new meaning
        to the wonder and MYSTERY OF LIFE!

...a little child shall lead them.

Isaiah 11:6

Remember These Words

We are gathered together
    on this happy day
To stand before God
    and to reverently say:
I take thee to be
    my partner for life,
To love and to live with
    as husband and wife;
To have and to hold
    forever, Sweetheart,
Through sickness and health
    until death do us part;
To love and to cherish
    whatever betide,
And in BETTER or WORSE
    to stand by your side...
We do this not lightly
    but solemnly, Lord,
Asking Thy blessing
    as we live in accord
With Thy Holy Precepts
    which join us in love
And assure us Thy guidance
    and grace from above...
And grant us, dear Lord,
    that "I WILL" and "I DO"
Are words that grow deeper
    and more meaningful, too,
Through long happy years
    of caring and sharing,
Secure in the knowledge
    that we are preparing
A love that is endless
    and never can die
But finds its fulfillment
    with YOU in the "SKY."

**And the Lord God said,
It is not good that the man should be alone;
I will make him an help meet for him.**

Genesis 2:18

But Jesus called them unto him, and said, Suffer little children to come unto me, and forbid them not: for of such is the kingdom of God. Verily I say unto you, Whosoever shall not receive the kingdom of God as a little child shall in no wise enter therein.

Luke 18:16, 17

A Child's Faith

"Jesus loves me, this I know,
      For the BIBLE tells me so"—
Little children ask no more,
      For love is all they're looking for,
And in a small child's shining eyes
      The FAITH of all the ages lies—
And tiny hands and tousled heads
      That kneel in prayer by little beds
Are closer to the dear LORD'S heart
      And of His Kingdom more a part
Than we who search, and never find,
      The answers to our questioning mind—
For FAITH in things we cannot see
      Requires a child's simplicity
For, lost in life's complexities,
      We drift upon uncharted seas
And slowly FAITH disintegrates
      While wealth and power accumulates—
And the more man learns, the less he knows,
      And the more involved his thinking grows
And, in his arrogance and pride,
      No longer is man satisfied
To place his confidence and love
      With childlike FAITH in God above—
Oh, Father, grant once more to men
      A simple childlike FAITH again
And, with a small child's trusting eyes,
      May all men come to realize
That FAITH alone can save man's soul
      And lead him to a HIGHER GOAL.

Trust in the Lord with all thine heart;
and lean not unto thine own understanding.

In all thy ways acknowledge him,
and he shall direct thy paths.

Happy is the man that findeth wisdom,
and the man that getteth understanding.

Proverbs 3:5, 6, 13

A Graduate's Prayer

Father, I have knowledge,
    So will You show me now
How to use it wisely
    And find a way somehow
To make the world I live in
    A little better place...
And make life with its problems
    A bit easier to face—
Grant me faith and courage
    And put purpose in my days—
And show me how to serve Thee
    In the most effective ways
So all my education,
    My knowledge and my skill,
May find their true fulfillment
    As I learn to do Thy Will.
And may I ever be aware
    In everything I do
That knowledge comes from learning—
    And wisdom comes from You.

With God As Your Partner

It takes a GROOM,
It takes a BRIDE,
TWO PEOPLE standing side by side...
It takes a RING
And VOWS that say
This is OUR HAPPY WEDDING DAY...
But marriage vows are sanctified
And loving hearts are unified
When standing with the bride and groom,
Unseen by others in the room,
The "SPIRIT OF THE LORD" is there
To bless this happy bridal pair...
For "GOD IS LOVE," and married life
Is richer for both man and wife
When God becomes a partner, too,
In everything they plan and do...
And every home is specially blest
When God is made a "DAILY GUEST."
For married folks who pray together
Are happy folks who stay together...
For when God's love becomes a part
Of body, mind, and soul and heart,
Their love becomes a wondrous blending
That's both ETERNAL and UNENDING,
And God looks down and says "well done"—
For now you TWO are truly ONE.

...every one that loveth is born of God....

1 John 4:7

Growing Older
Is Part of God's Plan

You can't "HOLD BACK THE DAWN"
Or "STOP THE TIDES FROM FLOWING" —
Or "KEEP A ROSE FROM WITHERING"
Or "STILL A WIND THAT'S BLOWING" —
And TIME CANNOT BE HALTED
      in its SWIFT and ENDLESS FLIGHT
For AGE is sure to follow YOUTH
      like DAY comes after NIGHT...
For HE who sets our span of years
      and watches from above
Replaces youth and beauty
      with PEACE and TRUTH and LOVE...
And then our souls are privileged
      to see a "HIDDEN TREASURE"
That in our youth escaped our eyes
      in OUR PURSUIT OF PLEASURE...
So BIRTHDAYS are but BLESSINGS
      that open up the way
To THE EVERLASTING BEAUTY
      of GOD'S ETERNAL DAY.

But the path of the just is as the shining light,
that shineth more and more unto the perfect day.

Proverbs 4:18

The Story of the Fire Lily

The crackling flames rise skyward
    As the waving grass is burned,
But from the fire on the veld
    A great truth can be learned...
For the green and living hillside
    Becomes a funeral pyre
As all the grass across the veld
    Is swallowed by the fire...
What yesterday was living,
    Today is dead and still,
But soon a breathless miracle
    Takes place upon the hill...
For, from the blackened ruins
    There arises life anew
And scarlet lilies lift their heads
    Where once the veld grass grew...
And so again the mystery
    Of life and death is wrought,
And man can find assurance
    In this soul-inspiring thought,
That from a bed of ashes
    The fire lilies grew,
And from the ashes of our lives
    God resurrects us, too.

...the dead shall hear the voice of the Son of God:
and they that hear shall live.

John 5:25

"I Know That My Redeemer Liveth"

They asked me how I know it's true
That the Saviour lived and died...
And if I believe the story
That the Lord was crucified?
And I have so many answers
To prove His Holy Being,
Answers that are everywhere
Within the realm of seeing...
The leaves that fell at Autumn
And were buried in the sod
Now budding on the tree boughs
To lift their arms to God...
The flowers that were covered
And entombed beneath the snow
Pushing through the "darkness"
To bid the Spring "hello"...
On every side Great Nature
Retells the Easter Story—
So who am I to question
"The Resurrection Glory."

For I know that my redeemer liveth, and that he shall
stand at the latter day upon the earth:

And though after my skin worms destroy this body,
yet in my flesh shall I see God.

Job 19:25, 26

Let not your heart be troubled:
ye believe in God, believe also in me.
In my Father's house are many mansions:
if it were not so, I would have told you.
I go to prepare a place for you.
And if I go and prepare a place for you,
I will come again, and receive you unto myself;
that where I am, there ye may be also.

John 14:1-3

When I Must Leave You

When I must leave you
     for a little while,
Please do not grieve
     and shed wild tears
And hug your sorrow
     to you through the years,
But start out bravely
     with a gallant smile;
And for my sake
     and in my name
Live on and do
     all things the same,
Feed not your loneliness
     on empty days,
But fill each waking hour
     in useful ways,
Reach out your hand
     in comfort and in cheer
And I in turn will comfort you
     and hold you near;
And never, never
     be afraid to die,
For I am waiting
     for you in the sky!

Death Opens the Door
to Life Evermore

We live a short while on earth below,
Reluctant to die for we do not know
Just what "dark death" is all about
And so we view it with fear and doubt
Not certain of what is around the bend
We look on death as the final end
To all that made us a mortal being
And yet there lies just beyond our seeing
A beautiful life so full and complete
That we should leave with hurrying feet
To walk with God by sacred streams
Amid beauty and peace beyond our dreams —
For all who believe in the RISEN LORD
Have been assured of this reward
And death for them is just "graduation"
To a higher realm of wide elevation —
For life on earth is a transient affair,
Just a few brief years in which to prepare
For a life that is free from pain and tears
Where time is not counted by hours or years —
For death is only the method God chose
To colonize heaven with the souls of those
Who by their apprenticeship on earth
Proved worthy to dwell in the land of new birth —
So death is not sad...it's a time for elation,
A joyous transition...the soul's emigration
Into a place where the soul's SAFE and FREE
To live with God through ETERNITY!

**...having a desire to depart,
and to be with Christ;
which is far better.**

Philippians 1:23

On the Other Side
of Death

Death is a GATEWAY
      we all must pass through
To reach that Fair Land
      where the soul's born anew,
For man's born to die
      and his sojourn on earth
Is a short span of years
      beginning with birth...
And like pilgrims we wander
      until death takes our hand
And we start on our journey
      to God's Promised Land,
A place where we'll find
      no suffering nor tears,
Where TIME is not counted
      by days, months or years...
And in this Fair City
      that God has prepared
Are unending joys
      to be happily shared
With all of our loved ones
      who patiently wait
On Death's Other Side
      to open "THE GATE"!

...Christ shall be magnified in my body,
whether it be by life, or by death.
For to me to live is Christ, and to die is gain.
For I am in a strait betwixt two,
having a desire to depart, and to be with Christ;
which is far better.

Philippians 1:20, 21, 23

With His Love

If you found any beauty
        in the poems in this book
Or some peace and comfort
        in a word or a line,
Don't give me the praise
        or worldly acclaim
For the words that you read
        are not mine...
I borrowed them all
        to share with you
From our
        HEAVENLY FATHER ABOVE,
And the joy that you felt
        was GOD speaking to you
As HE flooded your heart
        with HIS LOVE.

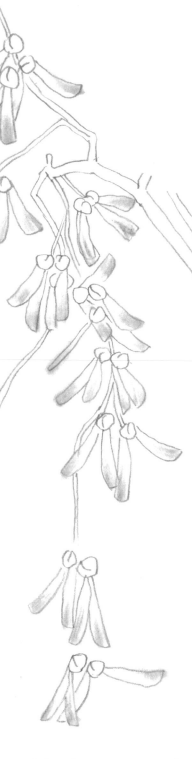

**Thy word is a lamp unto my feet,
and a light unto my path.**

Psalms 119:105